READ ABOUT
Helicopters

David Jefferis

WARWICK PRESS
New York/London/Toronto/Sydney

Published in 1990 by Warwick Press,
387 Park Avenue South, New York, New York 10016.
First published in 1989 by Kingfisher Books Ltd.
Copyright © Grisewood & Dempsey Ltd. 1989.

All rights reserved
5 4 3 2 1

Library of Congress Catalog Card No. 89-22543
ISBN 0-531-19069-2

Printed in Spain

Contents

Chopper Take-off! 4
Inside a Helicopter 6
Make a Heli-spinner 8
The Secret of Flight 10
Taking the Controls 12
Working Helicopters 14
At a Heliport 16
Rescue Mission 18
Attack Helicopters 20
Skycops and Skycranes 22
Into the Future 24
Heli-file 26
Glossary 30
Index 32

If you find an unusual or difficult word in this book, check for an explanation in the glossary on pages 30 and 31.

Chopper Take-off!

Stand by for your first ride in a helicopter! You are sitting beside the pilot in the cockpit, with a wide view out through its perspex bubble canopy. "Are you strapped in?" asks the pilot. You pull your seat belt a bit tighter, and nod your head. The engine rises to a hissing whine. Overhead, the rotor blades are spinning faster and faster, with a "whup-whup-whup" sound. They rapidly become a whizzing blur. Then the engine note deepens to a growl and your chopper soars skyward.

Inside a Helicopter

Although their design and mechanical details vary, all helicopters have a cockpit where the crew members sit. There is also an engine, of course — sometimes two or three.

Rotors are a helicopter's spinning "wings." Most have one main rotor on top, and a smaller one at the back to help steer. Some helicopters have two main rotors instead, turning in opposite directions.

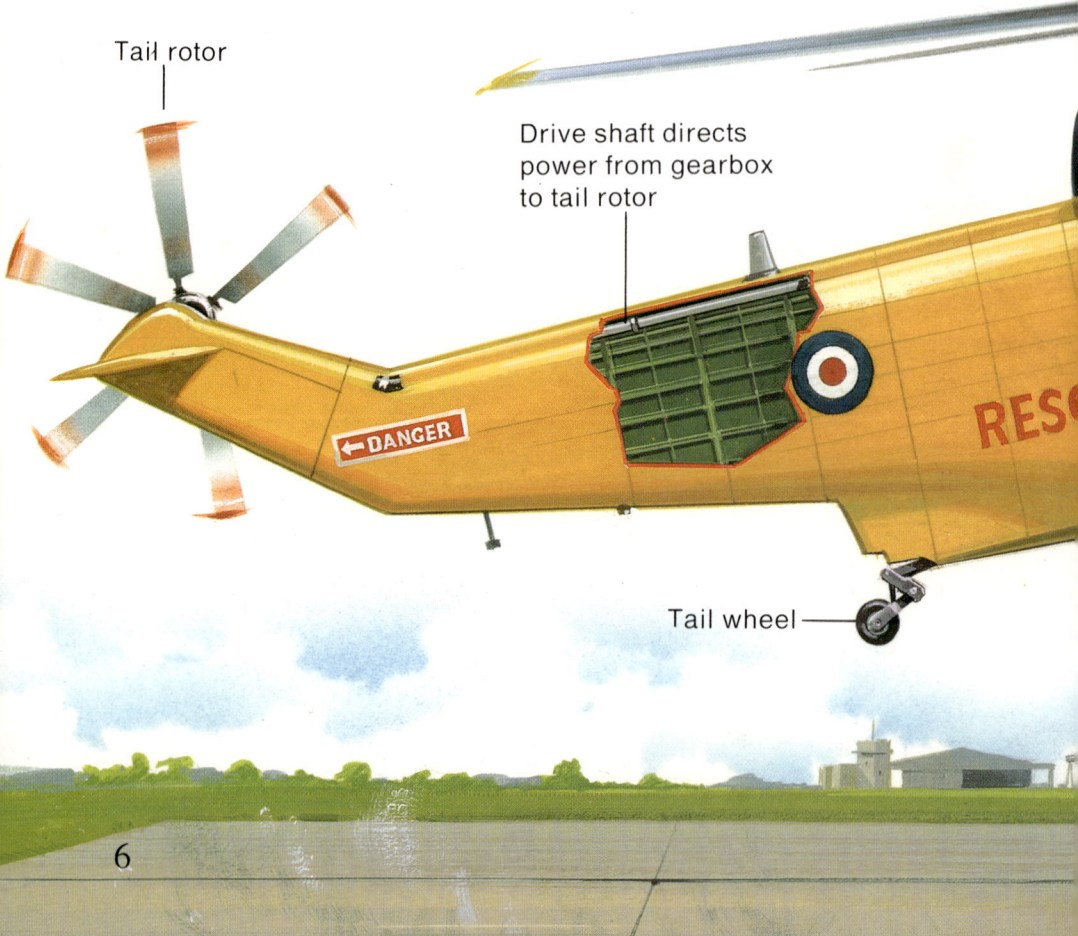

Tail rotor

Drive shaft directs power from gearbox to tail rotor

Tail wheel

CHOPPERS
Helicopters are nicknamed "choppers" or sometimes "egg-beaters" because of the way their rotors whirl and chop through the air. The machine below is a Sea King. It has two engines, a main rotor and a tail rotor. It is often used for rescues from the air.

Winch for air rescues

Gearbox

Main rotor

One of the Sea King's two engines

Cockpit

RESCUE

Cargo deck

Main wheel

An outrigger float on each side keeps the Sea King level if it makes an emergency landing in the sea

Make a Heli-spinner

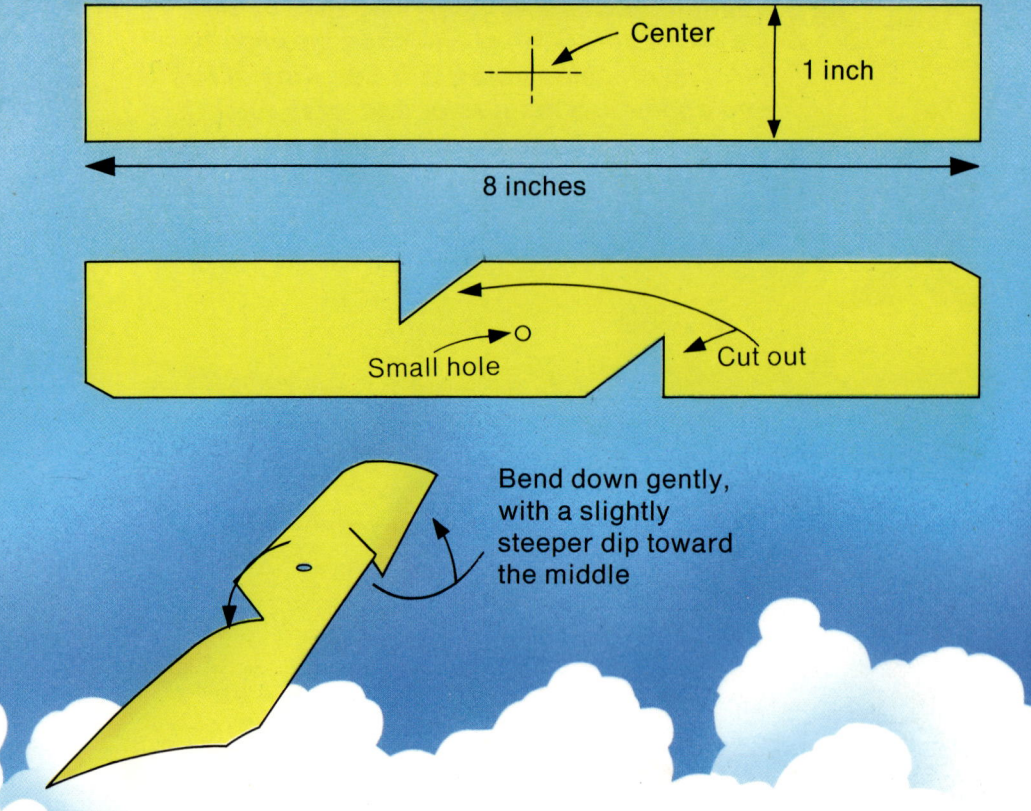

This model is easy to make and fun to fly. Use a pencil for the body and stiff cardboard for the rotor blades — ordinary postcard thickness is about right. Copy the above pattern onto the card, then make a small hole in the center and cut out the triangles. Bend the blades down, then push the pencil gently up through the hole. Glue the join and your spinner is ready for testing. Hold the bottom of the pencil between two fingers, flicking them to make it spin and lift off.

Pencil must have flat sides — a round one will slip

Glue the join

FLIGHT TESTING
Make a helicopter landing site by drawing a big letter H inside a circle on a large sheet of paper. Practice flicking your heli-spinner toward it, scoring ten if you land exactly on the H. Give yourself five for landing inside the circle, and three for outside it. Once you are scoring well, challenge your friends to a competition.

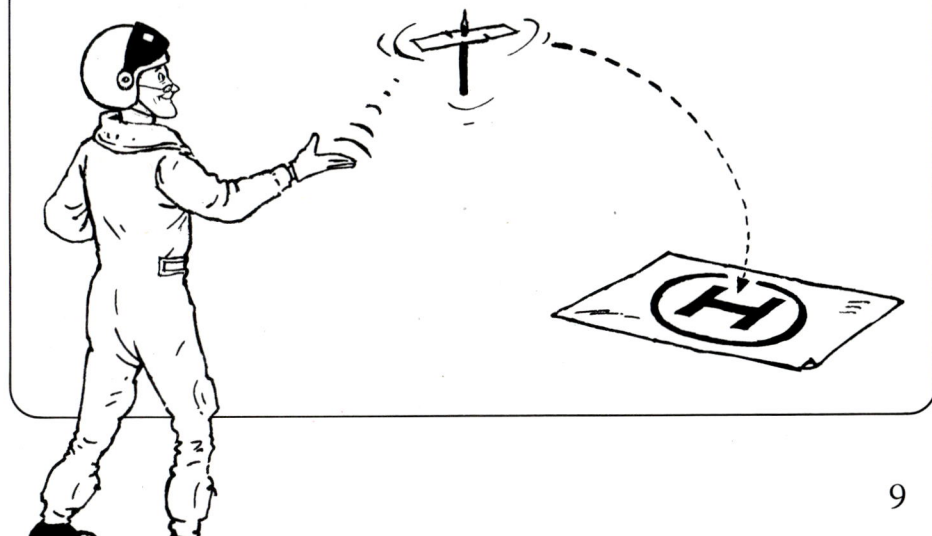

9

The Secret of Flight

Helicopters are kept airborne by the blades of their main rotor. As the blades turn, their rounded shape affects the way the air flows past them. The airflow produces an upward pull called "lift." The faster the blades turn, the greater the lift. When the lift is greater than its weight, the helicopter is pulled up into the air.

Fixed-wing aircraft have to move forward to get lift — that's why they speed down runways before takeoff. Because their main rotor gives them lift, choppers can take off anywhere and fly in any direction.

A lever called the collective pitch control varies the amount of lift produced by the main rotor. It is held with the left hand and pulled up or down to make the chopper fly upward or downward. It is also used as a "throttle" so as to adjust the engine power. Some throttles work automatically when the control is moved. Others are operated by twisting the top of the lever.

10

ROTOR LIFT

Moving the collective pitch control up and down changes the angle of the rotor blades. When they are flat, they spin without producing any lift. Pulling up on the collective pitch control angles the blades, so that they dig into the air to screw the chopper up into the sky.

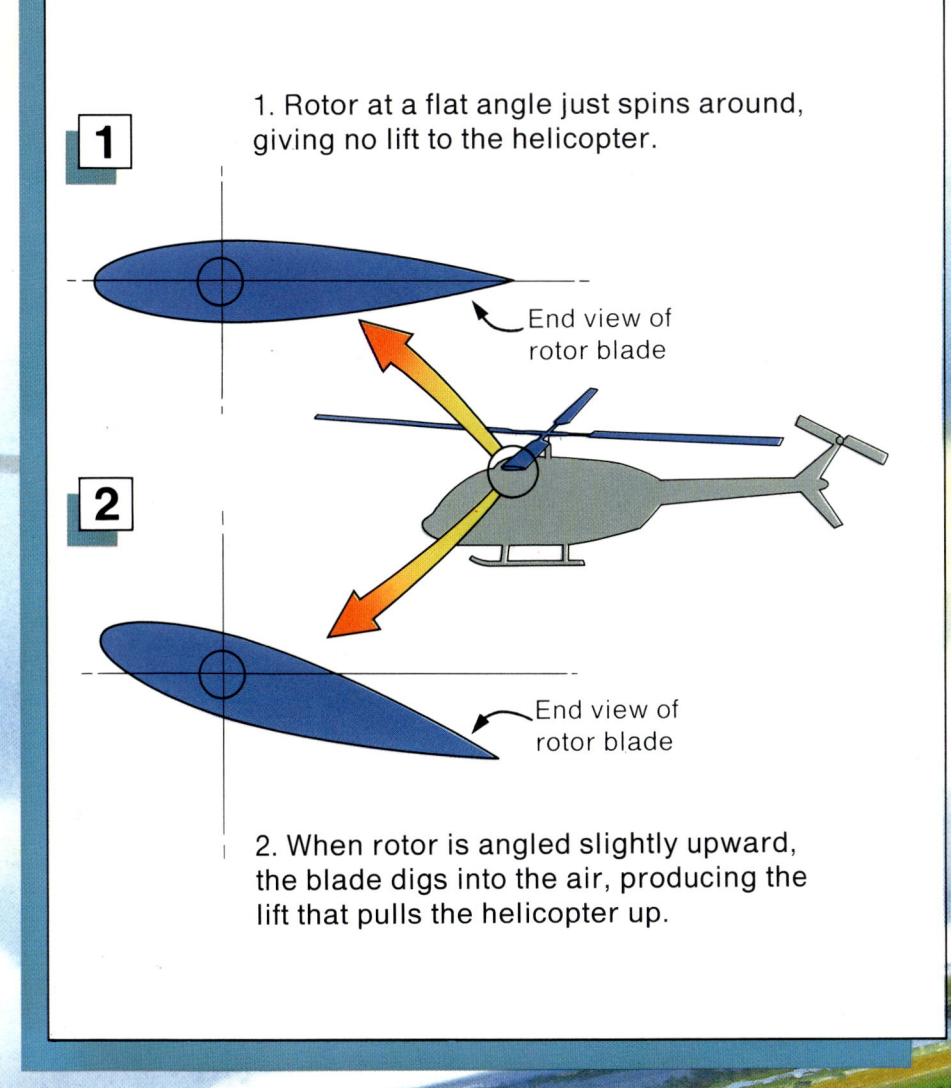

1. Rotor at a flat angle just spins around, giving no lift to the helicopter.

End view of rotor blade

2. When rotor is angled slightly upward, the blade digs into the air, producing the lift that pulls the helicopter up.

End view of rotor blade

Taking the Controls

Once in the air, a helicopter can be flown in any direction — up, down, forward, sideways — even backward! Flying needs constant attention, though. If you let go of the controls for more than a few seconds, your chopper will fall out of the sky.

Beside keeping an eye on the instrument dials and looking where you are going, you are operating the up-down collective pitch control with your left hand. You have the cyclic pitch control in your right hand and your feet are on the rudder pedals!

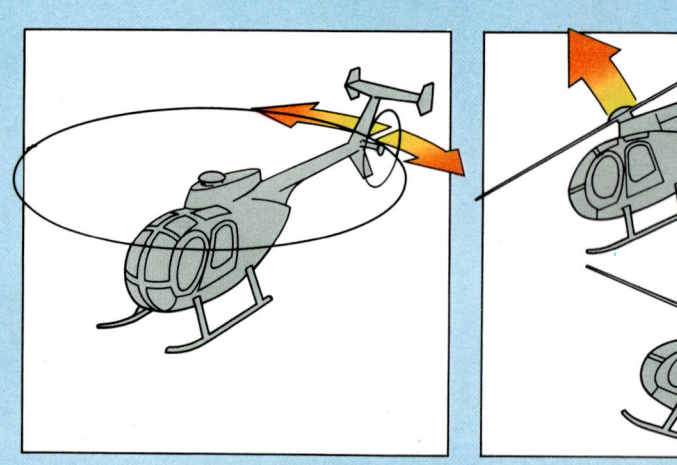

▲ The tail rotor swings the helicopter round to any compass heading, as well as stopping it from spinning out of control in the same circle as the main rotor. Rudder pedals control the tail rotor, and they are operated by the feet.

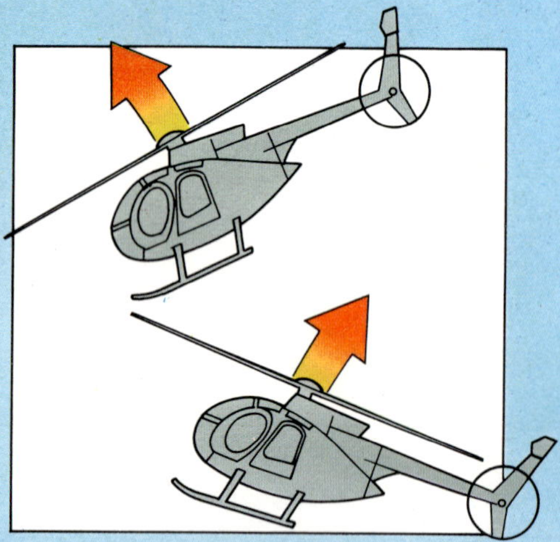

▲ The cyclic pitch control tilts the main rotor forward, backward or sideways to direct the helicopter's flight — angling the rotor forward sends the chopper straight ahead, and so on. It is operated by the pilot's right hand.

IN THE COCKPIT

This is a two-seat AH-64 Apache. It is armed with guns, rockets, and missiles and is used as a deadly "tank-killer" weapon. The crew sit one behind the other, with the pilot in the raised rear seat. Below you can see the position of the flight controls.

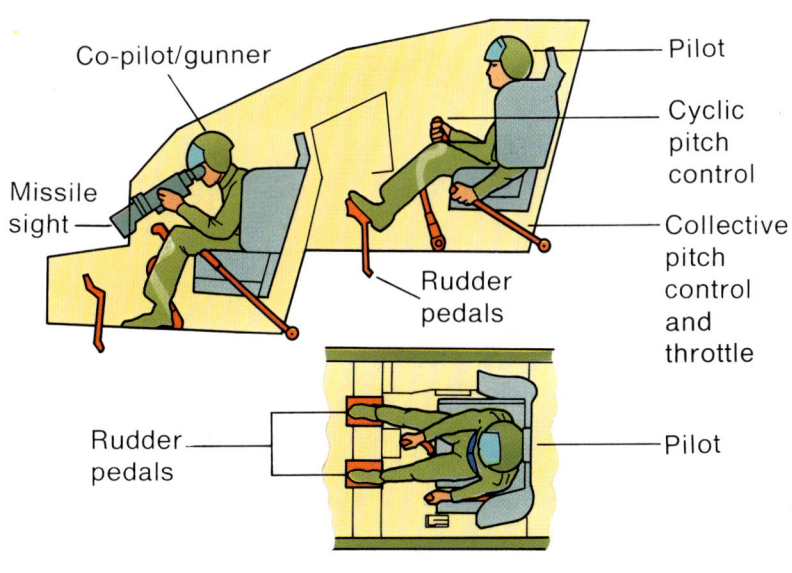

Working Helicopters

Choppers come in many different shapes and sizes, and are used in all sorts of different jobs. Small ones are often used as traffic spotters by the police, for instance, or as high-speed transport for business people in a hurry. The bigger choppers take more passengers and carry more fuel. They are often used to carry cargo or people over longer distances, such as flying workers out to oil rigs at sea. Big or small, the advantage helicopters have over fixed-wing aircraft is that they don't need a runway.

Alouette III, often used by the police

MBB Bo 105, here used as an ambulance

Sikorsky S-55, a medium-size helicopter, used by both business and the military

Boeing 243, can carry over 40 passengers

SOUND BOUNCER

Choppers vibrate a lot and are noisy to fly in, due to the sound of the engine and spinning rotors. This tends to loosen up such things as nuts and bolts, so engineers have to check very carefully between flights. This experiment shows just how powerful sound vibrations are at making things move — it's almost like magic!

1: Stretch a piece of kitchen plastic film across the top of a jelly-jar and secure it with a rubber band.

2: Sprinkle some sugar on the plastic film.

3: Hold a tin container near the jar and bang it with a wooden spoon. The sugar will leap into the air, bounced by the sound vibrations.

At a Heliport

How would you like to ride in a helicopter as a passenger? You would have to go to a heliport, which is a smaller version of the giant airports used by big jet planes. The helicopters are kept in a big garage called a hangar, and the parking area outside it is called the apron. There usually isn't a long runway, just an H in a circle to mark the spot where the choppers take off and land.

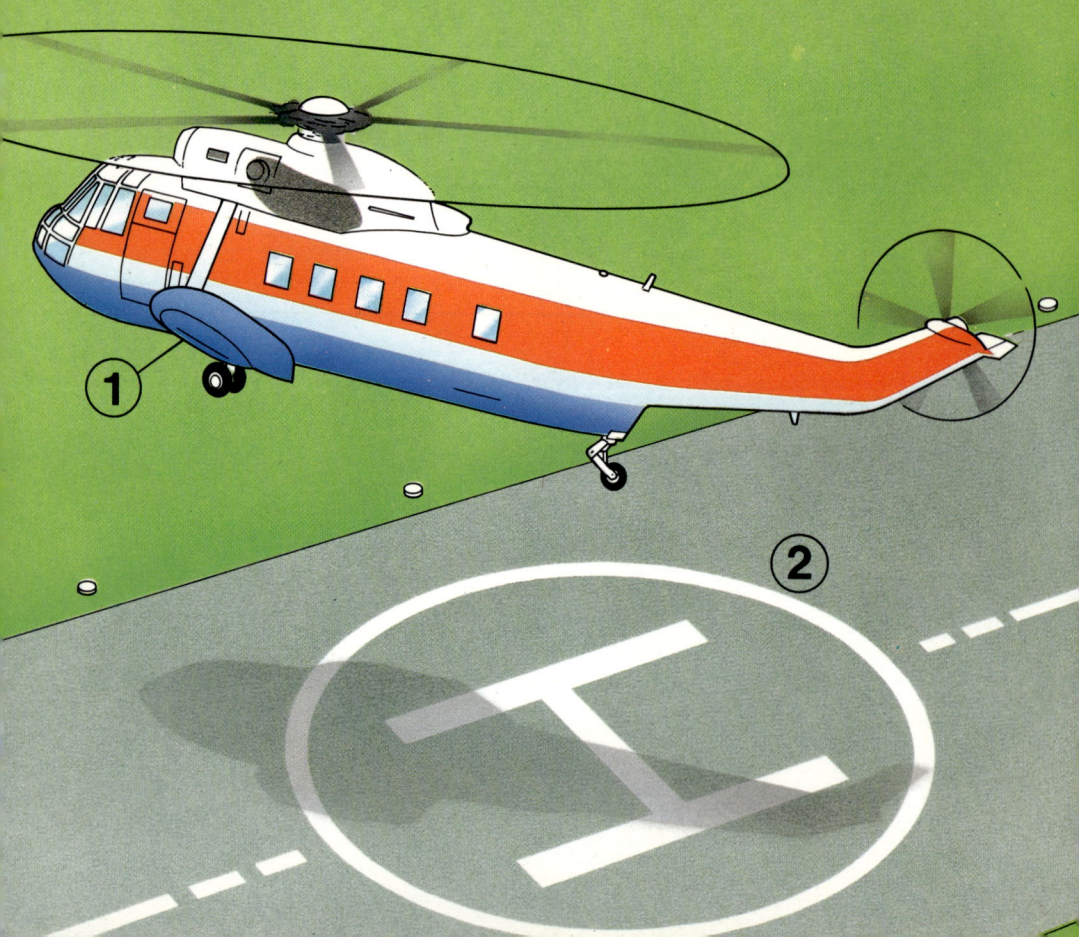

KEY

1: Helicopters lift off and land vertically (upward and downward), so they don't need runways.
2: The apron is clearly marked with an H on the spot where choppers take off and land.
3: The hangar is where the choppers are kept.
4: Engineers service the machines between flights.
5: Tools and equipment are also stored in the hangar.
6: A windsock shows the direction and strength of the wind.
7: The fire crew and truck are ready for emergencies.
8: The terminal building has check-in desks inside, where passengers show their tickets before boarding their chopper.

Rescue Mission

Thousands of crashed aircraft crews and shipwrecked sailors have been saved using air-sea rescue helicopters. Only choppers have the ability to hover over one spot while people are hauled out of the water straight up into them.

The world's busiest air-sea rescue station is at Miami, Florida. Its coastguard pilots fly Dolphin helicopters on about 800 rescue missions each year. This is the story of one of those flights.

▲ A man slips on the deck of his boat and falls overboard. Some time later the empty boat is spotted by another sailor, who alerts the coastguard by radio.

▶ A pair of Dolphin helicopters take off from Miami, heading for the area where the boat was last seen.

▲ The Dolphin crews look out for the missing sailor as they fly low over the sea.

▶ The man is spotted — luckily he is still alive and can climb into a rescue cage, which is lowered to him on a strong steel cable. One more life saved!

19

Attack Helicopters

Military helicopters are used for transporting weapons and carrying soldiers, as well as looking out for the enemy. Special attack choppers are used against enemy tanks. Flying very low, the pilot sneaks toward the enemy using hills, trees, and buildings as cover. When he is near, he pulls his chopper up out of cover, takes aim and fires off a missile, then whirls off to hunt for another target.

Some choppers have a periscope sight mounted above the main rotor. This allows a pilot to take aim (1) while his machine is hidden. He pops up, fires a missile (2), and then sinks back down into cover once again.

MAKE A PERISCOPE

With this periscope you'll be able to see over walls and around corners! As well as a sheet of stiff cardboard, you'll need two small mirrors, the same size. Don't make your periscope too long, or it will be floppy.

◀ Draw this pattern on to cardboard and cut it out. Cut out the square hole at the top. Fold the cardboard and glue the angled mirrors top and bottom, reflective sides facing.

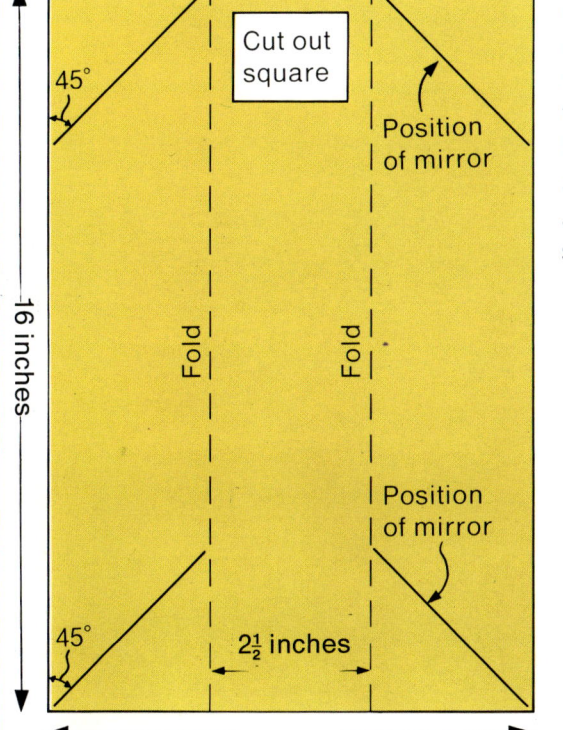

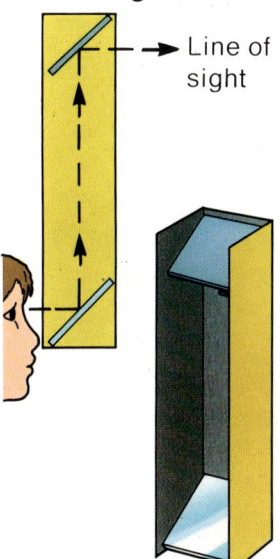

Skycops and Skycranes

Because they can hover, fly slowly, and turn easily, helicopters have many uses. The police use them to spot traffic jams, report accidents, and look for criminals. Powerful searchlights turn choppers into perfect night hunters. As a police pilot, you would flick the searchlight across the dark streets below you. In its white light, even the darkest alley looks as bright as day. If you spot a criminal, you can pin him down in the searchlight's glare while you radio for ground forces to make an arrest!

▲ Choppers are often used as flying cranes. The big Boeing Chinook has two main rotors and can lift a 12-ton load with its underbelly cargo hook.

▶ Hovering over the scene of the crime, these police officers use the searchlights of their Bell helicopter to guide the ground forces to the criminal.

Into the Future

The Osprey is a machine which can take off like a helicopter, but fly like a plane. It has a pair of tilt-rotors, mounted one at the end of each wing. These work like a helicopter's main rotor to lift the helicopter directly up into the air. Once the Osprey is airborne, however, its tilt-rotors swing down and act like the propellers of a normal aircraft — powering it to speeds twice as fast as those reached by most helicopters. The first Ospreys are being built for use on aircraft carriers.

CITY-CENTER AIRLINER
Since they don't need the runways that big jets must have for takeoff and landing, tilt-rotor airliners may one day fly passengers between city-center heliports.

Heli-file

Many different helicopters fly with the world's armed forces and airlines. The three below are military choppers — you might see them at an air show.

EH.101

Westland Lynx

Bell 205 Iroquois

PAINTED DISGUISES

Military helicopters are usually painted to blend in with their background. This is called camouflage, and the colors change according to where a chopper is used. In desert lands, sandy colors can be chosen. For forests, camouflage is based on shades of green.

▼ Desert colors

▲ Northern Europe colors

▲ Sea gray, used on navy choppers

Try camouflaging you own chopper. Trace off copies of this machine and paint them for different countries. How would you camouflage a helicopter for snowy Switzerland, for instance?

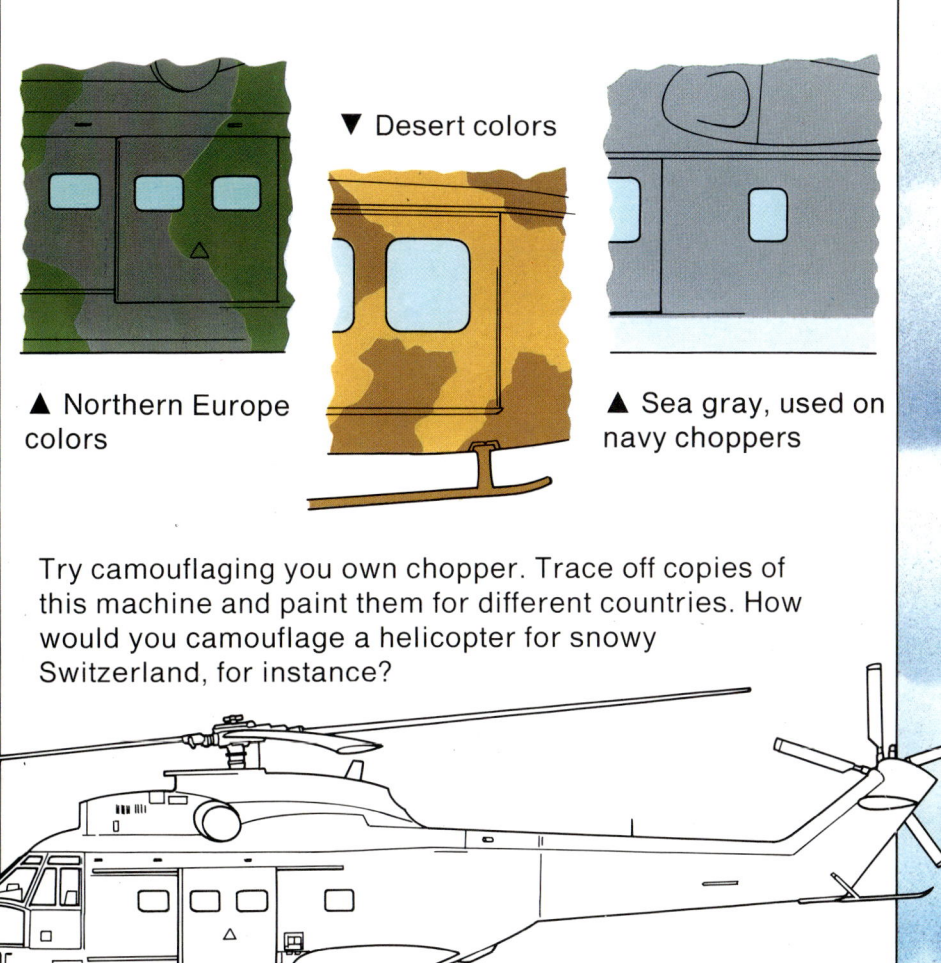

Heli-file – 2

Sikorsky Seahawk, used by the U.S. Navy

Robinson R22, used for training as it is cheap and simple to fly

DESIGN A CHOPPER

Helicopters have three basic layouts. The most popular is the single main rotor and small tail rotor, but some choppers have two main rotors. One layout puts the rotors one above the other. Try sketching designs of your own with these basic layouts in mind.

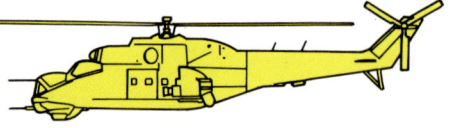

Mil Mi-24 — single main rotor

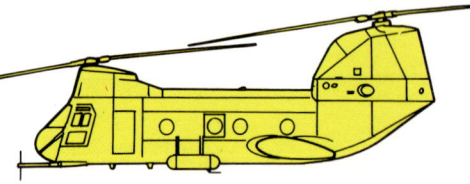

Boeing/Kawasaki KV-107 — twin rotors

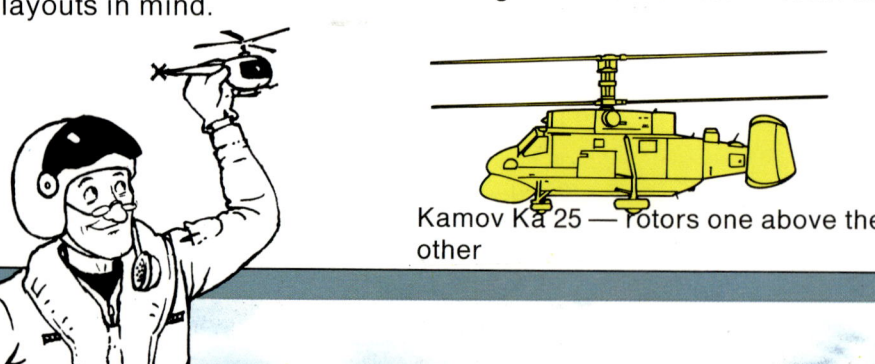

Kamov Ka 25 — rotors one above the other

Aérospatiale Dauphin, a French-made helicopter

BK 117, a German-Japanese model

Here are some design ideas to inspire you:

Fighter heliplane

Company helijet

"Flying crane" heli-lifter

29

Glossary

Aircraft carrier
Large flat-topped ship, built as a floating airfield. The biggest aircraft carriers can take over 100 planes.

Apron
Concrete area in front of the hangar or terminal buildings. An H in a circle often marks the spot where helicopters take off and land.

Blades
Long thin parts of a rotor, which give a helicopter lift when spinning at an angle.

Bubble canopy
Curved windshield used on many helicopters, especially small ones, to give a wide view out of the cockpit.

Camouflage
Method of disguise used on military equipment such as helicopters, tanks and jet planes, to stop them showing against a background. Usually, paint schemes are chosen which blend in with the surrounding landscape.

Coastguard
People who look after shipping near the coast.

Cockpit
The area where the crew sit. Seats, instruments, and flight controls are all in the cockpit.

Collective pitch control
One of a helicopter pilot's flight controls. This angles the main rotor to control lift and give up-down motion.

Cyclic pitch control
One of a helicopter pilot's flight controls. This tilts the main rotor to give forward, backward or sideways motion.

Drive shaft and gearbox
Spinning rod and gear system which directs power from the helicopter's engine to the main and tail rotors.

Fixed-wing aircraft
Unlike a helicopter, these have wings that are fixed to the body of the aircraft.

30

Flight controls
The controls a pilot uses to fly a helicopter.

Hangar
Large building used for storage and servicing of aircraft.

Lift
The upward force that supports the weight of a helicopter in the air. The spinning blades of the main rotor give lift.

Rotor
The blades and rotor head which join to form a helicopter's spinning wings.

Rudder pedals
One of a helicopter pilot's flight controls. These are used to control the tail rotor for steering.

Runway
Long, concrete strip used for takeoff and landing by fixed-wing aircraft.

Tail rotor
Helicopters that have a single main rotor need another smaller rotor to help steer them, otherwise they would spin in the same direction as the main rotor blades. The tail rotor is operated by the rudder pedals.

Terminal
The main building at an airport or heliport, through which passengers go to board a flight or after the flight is over.

Twin-rotor helicopters
Some machines have a pair of main rotors — one at the front and the other at the back. These spin in opposite directions — clockwise and counter-clockwise. This avoids the spinning motion that a single main rotor gives to a helicopter, so twin-rotor choppers do not need a separate tail rotor.

Windsock
This is an open-ended fabric tube hoisted on a flagpole. Because the wind blows it back, it shows the wind's direction. In a strong wind it lifts to become parallel to the ground. When the wind is weak it hangs limply.

Index

Aérospatiale Dauphin 29
AH-64 Apache 13
aircraft carriers 24, 30
Alouette III 14
apron 16, 30

Bell 205 Iroquois 26
BK 117 29
Boeing 243 14
Boeing Chinook 22
Boeing/Kawasaki KV-107 28

camouflage 27, 30
coastguard 18–19, 30
cockpit 6, 7, 13, 30
collective pitch control 10, 11, 12, 13, 30
cyclic pitch control 12, 13, 30

Dolphin 18–19
drive shaft 6, 30

EH.101 26
engine 6, 7

flight controls 10–13, 31

Gazelle 4–5
gearbox 7, 30

hangar 16, 17, 31

heliport 16–17

Kamov Ka 25 28

lift 10, 11, 31

military helicopters 5, 20, 26
Mil Mi-24 28

Osprey 24–5

police helicopters 14, 22–3

rescue, air-sea 6–7, 18–19
Robinson R22 28
rotor, main 7, 10, 11, 20, 28, 31
  tail 6, 12, 28, 31
  tilt 24–5
  twin 14, 22, 28, 31
rudder pedals 12, 13, 31
runway 31

Sea King 6–7
Sikorsky S-55 14
Sikorsky Seahawk 28

terminal 17, 31
throttle 10, 31
traffic helicopters 14
transport helicopters 14, 22

weapons 13, 20
Westland Lynx 26
windsock 17, 31

32